RESEARCH TOOLS YOU CAN USE

How Do I Use an Encyclopedia?

Suzanne Weinick

Britannica
Educational Publishing
IN ASSOCIATION WITH

ROSEN
EDUCATIONAL SERVICES

Published in 2015 by Britannica Educational Publishing (a trademark of Encyclopædia Britannica, Inc.) in association with The Rosen Publishing Group, Inc.
29 East 21st Street, New York, NY 10010

Distributed exclusively by Rosen Publishing.
To see additional Britannica Educational Publishing titles, go to rosenpublishing.com.

First Edition

Britannica Educational Publishing
J.E. Luebering: Director, Core Reference Group
Mary Rose McCudden: Editor, Britannica Student Encyclopedia

Rosen Publishing
Hope Lourie Killcoyne: Executive Editor
Nicholas Croce: Editor
Nelson Sá: Art Director
Nicole Russo: Designer
Cindy Reiman: Photography Manager
Cindy Reiman: Photo Researcher

Cataloging-in-Publication Data

Weinick, Suzanne.
How do I use an encyclopedia?/Suzanne Weinick.
    pages cm.—(Research tools you can use)
Includes bibliographical references and index.
ISBN 978-1-62275-384-0 (library bound)—ISBN 978-1-62275-386-4 (pbk.)—ISBN 978-1-62275-387-1 (6-pack)
1. Children's encyclopedias and dictionaries. 2. English language—Encyclopedias, Juvenile. 3. English language—Encyclopedias—Juvenile literature. I. Title.
AG5.W447 2014
031—dc23

2014003043

Manufactured in the United States of America

Photo credits:
Cover and interior pages (background) © iStockphoto.com/Ulrich Knaupe; cover (inset from left) lightpoet/Shutterstock.com, © iStockphoto.com/Kali Nine LLC, Jetta Productions/Digital Visions/Thinkstock; p. 4 Mario Tama/Getty Images; pp. 6, 7, 8, 13, 17 Used with permission Encyclopædia Britannica Online, copyright 2014, by Encyclopædia Britannica, Inc.; p. 10 Brand X Pictures/Stockbyte/Getty Images; p. 11 traveler1116/E+/Getty Images; p. 14 Todd Warnock/Digital Vision/Thinkstock; p. 16 KidStock/Blend Images/Getty Images; p. 19 Image Source/Digital Vision/Getty Images; p. 20 LuminaStock/iStock/Thinkstock; p. 21 xamnesiacx/Shutterstock.com; p. 22 Fuse/Getty Images; p. 23 wavebreakmedia/Shutterstock.com; p. 24 © AP Images; p. 25 Alina Solovyova-Vincent/E+/Getty Images; p. 26 © Michael Newman/PhotoEdit; p. 28 Peter Dazeley/The Image Bank/Getty Images.

TABLE OF CONTENTS

CHAPTER 1

What Is an Encyclopedia?

An encyclopedia is a good place to start when you are trying to learn about a new topic.

An encyclopedia is a resource that contains information on many different subjects or that provides in-depth information on one particular subject. Most are reliable sources of information because their content is reviewed and checked by professionals for its accuracy.

It doesn't matter if you are doing a project or report for school or if you are just seeking more information about a sports figure, animal, place in the world, or event that happened in history. Encyclopedias provide a wealth of information in the form of articles, photographs, illustrations, maps, tables, and many other elements. You can explore the world around you without leaving your home or school by using an encyclopedia.

PRINT AND ONLINE ENCYCLOPEDIAS

Encyclopedias are available in two formats: print and online. Before computers, an encyclopedia

Encyclopædia Britannica
See Full Size

First edition of the *Encyclopædia Britannica*.

Credit, Links and Citations

Credit	Encyclopædia Britannica, Inc.
Links	• encyclopaedia (reference work) • Encyclopædia Britannica (English language reference work) • Encyclopædia Britannica (print encyclopaedia)
Citations	**MLA style:** *Encyclopædia Britannica.* Photograph. *Encyclopædia Britannica Online.* Web. 14 Feb. 2014. <http://www.britannica.com/EBchecked/media/97337/First-edition-of-the-Encyclopaedia-Britannica>. **APA style:** *Encyclopædia Britannica.* [Photograph]. In *Encyclopædia Britannica.* Retrieved from http://www.britannica.com/EBchecked/media/97337/First-edition-of-the-Encyclopaedia-Britannica **Harvard style:**

Encyclopedias are available in both print and online versions.

USING AN ENCYCLOPEDIA TO RESEARCH THE MOON

What if you want to learn about the moon? Here is what an encyclopedia might say about it: "The moon is a large natural object that orbits, or travels around, Earth. After the sun, it is the brightest object in the sky. The average distance between the moon and Earth is about 238,600 miles (384,000 kilometers)."

was a printed collection of articles organized in alphabetical order by topic. The articles could be contained in a single volume or in many volumes. An online encyclopedia has the same information as a print version, but it has many additional features.

Britannica ACADEMIC EDITION

Hubble Space Telescope (HST) | Go | Advanced Search

Table of Contents | EDIT | SAVE | PRINT | E-MAIL

Video, Images & Audio

VIDEOS

Related Articles, Ebooks & More

Web Links

Article History

Contributors

Dictionary & Thesaurus

IMAGES

Workspace

Widgets

Hubble Space Telescope (HST)

ARTICLE *from the Encyclopædia Britannica* | Get Involved | Share | Like | 0 | g+1

Hubble Space Telescope (HST), the most sophisticated optical observatory ever placed into orbit around Earth. Earth's atmosphere obscures ground-based astronomers' view of celestial objects by absorbing or distorting light rays from them. A telescop stationed in outer **space** is entirely above the atmosphere, however, and receives images of much greater brightness, clarity, and de than do ground-based telescopes with comparable optics.

After the U.S. Congress had authorized its construction in 1977, the **Hubble Space** Telescope was built under the supervision of the National Aeronautics and Space Administration (NASA) of the United States and was named after Edwin Hubble, the foremost Am astronomer of the 20th century. The HST was placed into orbit about 600 km (370 miles) above Earth by the crew of the space shutt *Discovery* on April 25, 1990.

The HST is a large reflecting telescope whose mirror optics gather light from celestial objects and direct it into two cameras and two spectrographs. The HST has a 2.4-metre (94-inch) primary mirror, a smaller secondary mirror, and various recording instruments that detect visible, ultraviolet, and infrared light. The most important of these instruments, the wide-field planetary camera, can take eithe field or high-resolution images of the planets and of galactic and extragalactic objects. This camera is designed to achieve image resolutions 10 times greater than that of even the largest Earth-based telescope. A faint-object camera can detect an object 50 times than anything observable by any ground-based telescope; a faint-object spectrograph gathers data on the object's chemical compos high-resolution spectrograph receives distant objects' ultraviolet light that cannot reach Earth because of atmospheric absorption.

About one month after launch, it became apparent that the HST's large primary mirror had been ground to the wrong shape owing to testing procedures by the mirror's manufacturer. The resulting optical defect, spherical aberration, caused the mirror to produce fuzzy than sharp images. The HST also developed problems with its gyroscopes and with its solar-power arrays. On December 2–13, 199 mission of the NASA space shuttle *Endeavour* sought to correct the telescope's optical system and other problems. In five **space** wa shuttle astronauts replaced the HST's wide-field planetary camera and installed a new device containing 10 tiny mirrors to correct the paths from the primary mirror to the other three scientific instruments. The mission proved an unqualified success, and the HST soon operating at its full potential, returning spectacular photographs of various cosmic phenomena.

Three subsequent **space** shuttle missions in 1997, 1999, and 2002 repaired the HST's gyroscopes and added new instruments in

Online encyclopedias are easy to use and sometimes give you more information than print encyclopedias.

00:09 ▮▮ ─────────── 01:07

▶	00:09 ▬■		01:07	◀◀

Caption Credit Links Citations

You can view video footage on a topic through an online encyclopedia.

These can include audio and video clips, interactive atlases and other tools, and built-in dictionaries.

Online encyclopedias have almost unlimited space, so they can contain more information than a printed encyclopedia can contain. They are also updated frequently.

CHAPTER 2

Searching an Encyclopedia

An encyclopedia is a good place to start when doing research on a topic. A general encyclopedia can help you make connections between different topics. It can also help you narrow down a topic for a project. If you know what subject you want to research, you can use an encyclopedia on a particular topic, such as an encyclopedia of dogs.

SEARCHING A PRINT ENCYCLOPEDIA

Print encyclopedias are a good place to start your research.

If you are interested in aardvarks, search for the word "aardvark" in the encyclopedia, starting with the letter "A" in the printed version of an encyclopedia. The entries are listed in alphabetical order.

The encyclopedia will tell you that an aardvark is an animal. It will give a brief description of the animal. It may also have a picture of an aardvark so that you will know what it looks like.

The entry might say something like: "Aardvarks live in dry places in Africa south of the Sahara Desert. The aardvark can reach a length of 6 feet (1.8 meters). Its head has huge donkey-like ears, a long snout, and drooping eyelids with long lashes."

Encyclopedias often have photographs and illustrations, which help you see what you are researching.

If you are searching for a person, look up the person's last name in the encyclopedia.

SEARCHING AN ONLINE ENCYCLOPEDIA

An online encyclopedia can be used to find the same information about an aardvark. The difference is that you will type the **search term** "aardvark" in the search box. The search results will provide a listing of articles that have the word "aardvark."

A proper search can lead you

A **search term** is a word or a phrase used to search for information online. It is typed within the search box on a website.

Online encyclopedias will list all articles that contain the search term you type in the search box. The more search terms you enter in the search box, the more narrow and focused your search will be.

When you search for a term, the results will appear in a list.

to a lot of information. It is important to know that with online searches, you should try to be as specific as possible about what you

ONLINE ENCYCLOPEDIAS

Online encyclopedias often provide more information than print encyclopedia volumes. Online encyclopedias can also search abbreviations of terms. You may be able to find information on Franklin Delano Roosevelt, the 32nd president of the United States, by entering "FDR" in the search box.

are looking for. You should also make sure you spell your search term correctly.

Encyclopedias enhance your knowledge and provide you with a resource for lifelong learning.

CHAPTER 3

Finding Related Information

Both print and online encyclopedias have features that allow the user to find additional information and related topics for each article.

TABLE OF CONTENTS

In an online encyclopedia, a **table of contents** provides an outline of the sections of the article.

A **table of contents** is a list of the main sections of an encyclopedia entry.

The table of contents makes it easy to find what you're looking for within the article. It also makes it easy to quickly see what the article is about.

You may find related information at the end of each encyclopedia article.

This will help you focus your search by allowing you to click on specific topics related to your subject. The table of contents will also help you understand how the article is organized.

CROSS-REFERENCES

Cross-references are words or phrases in an online encyclopedia that are in bold print,

FINDING RELATED INFORMATION

Online encyclopedias highlight topics and articles related to what you are currently studying.

underlined, or highlighted. Each cross-reference is linked to another article. Cross-references give the reader more information about the subject in another area of the encyclopedia.

OTHER RESOURCES

Some encyclopedia articles have a bibliography at the end. A bibliography is a list of books

Cross-references show you where you can find more information on a topic. They can be found in all types of encyclopedias.

In online encyclopedias, the cross-references are usually within the text of the article or at the end of the article. They usually appear as links. You can click on a link and be taken to that article.

In print encyclopedias, cross-references usually appear within the text as notes telling you to "see," or look up, an article that is similar or has more information on the subject.

or other sources that can provide more information about the topic.

Online encyclopedias also may have links to related websites and media.

Use a dictionary to look up new or unfamiliar words that you may find in an encyclopedia.

CHAPTER 4

Additional Research

Take notes on the information you find through your research and put the ideas into your own words.

It is not enough to just use an encyclopedia to find information on a subject. You must also understand what the information means and be able to put it into your own words. In addition, you must consult other sources. Your teacher may have rules about how many sources you must use for each assignment.

Newspapers are great for finding more information about your chosen topic.

USING OTHER SOURCES

Using an encyclopedia is just the beginning of the research process. The information you find in an encyclopedia must be combined with other research. The additional sources may be a dictionary, an atlas, other books, or an Internet search. Each of these can provide new information, or they can give a different view of the subject.

Doing additional research can help you verify your findings.

DOUBLE-CHECK YOUR SOURCES

The Internet is a wonderful source of information. However, not all information on the Internet is useful or appropriate. It is important that you ask a parent, teacher, or librarian about what websites are appropriate for you to go to for information.

In addition, not everything found on the Internet is factually correct. Therefore, you should always check at least two other sources to make sure the information you receive from the Internet is accurate.

Periodicals such as newspapers and magazines are also sources that can be used to find more information after you complete an encyclopedia search. These sources are frequently updated. They may have information on a topic that is not yet in books.

Libraries provide a variety of research sources, including books, newspapers, magazines, and other periodicals.

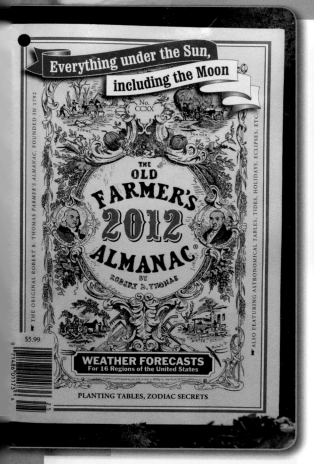

The Old Farmer's Almanac has been published since 1792.

An **almanac** is a resource. It is a book containing a calendar of days, weeks, and months. It may also include facts about the rising and setting of the sun and moon, changes in the tides, and information of general interest.

An almanac is a good additional resource to use to find information that may not be in an encyclopedia.

Almanacs, which are books published each year that contain important statistics, are another great resource to use when doing research. You can find them in your school or local public library. They contain fun facts on topics that may interest you.

CHAPTER 5

Good Research Skills

Good research skills are learned over time. You learn them by using a variety of sources to find answers to your questions.

It is helpful to make an outline or a list of facts you gather while doing your research. You will need to organize your information in a way that makes sense for the project or assignment you are given by your teacher.

If you have trouble beginning your research, your librarian is a great person to talk to.

Taking notes on index cards makes it easy to organize the notes later.

RESEARCH

Research is the collecting of information about a subject for the purpose of discovering and explaining new knowledge.

When a teacher assigns you to research a topic or subject, you should start by asking, "What question do I need to answer?"

The second step is to use an encyclopedia to get basic information to answer that question.

The third step is to write down the information you have collected and put it into your own words. The fourth step is to look at other sources and take notes from that. The fifth step is to organize all of the notes that you took from the various sources you used. When you have organized the information and read all of it over, you can

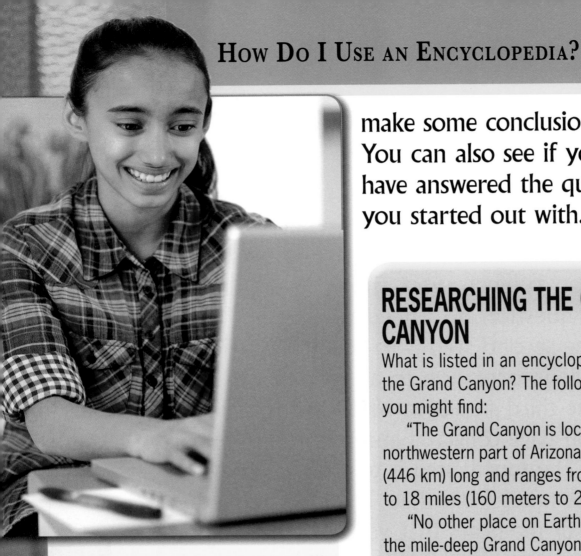

make some conclusions. You can also see if you have answered the question you started out with.

Practicing your research skills will help open you up to worlds of new information.

RESEARCHING THE GRAND CANYON

What is listed in an encyclopedia about the Grand Canyon? The following is what you might find:

"The Grand Canyon is located in the northwestern part of Arizona. It is 277 miles (446 km) long and ranges from 175 yards to 18 miles (160 meters to 29 km) wide.

"No other place on Earth compares with the mile-deep Grand Canyon for its record of geological events. Some of the canyon's rocks date back about 4 billion years."

ACTIVITY: TEST YOUR RESEARCH SKILLS

A great way to test your research skills is to ask a question. Then use an encyclopedia and other sources to find the answer to that question.

Here are some questions to test your use of an encyclopedia:

- Who was the 28th president of the United States?
- What years was he in office?
- What were his most famous accomplishments?

atlas A collection of maps that provide facts about continents, countries, states, and cities.

Internet An electronic communications network that connects computers around the world.

link Also known as a hyperlink, an electronic way to make a direct connection from one document on a website to another.

multimedia Using or composed of more than one form of communication or expression.

research The collection of information about a subject.

resource Something that can be used to find information.

BOOKS

Asselin, Kristine Carlson. *Smart Research Strategies*. North Mankato, MN: Capstone Press, 2013.

Bodden, Valerie. *Doing Primary Research*. Mankato, MN: The Creative Company, 2012.

Gallion, Sue Lowell. *Rick and Rachel Build a Research Report* (Writing Builders). Chicago, IL: Norwood House Press, 2013.

Owings, Lisa. *Do Your Research* (Library Smarts). Minneapolis, MN: Lerner, 2013.

Throp, Claire. *Put It Together: Using Information* (Our World of Information). Portsmouth, NH: Heinemann, 2009.

WEBSITES

Because of the changing nature of Internet links, Rosen Publishing has developed an online list of websites related to the subject of this book. This site is updated regularly. Please use this link to access the list:

http://www.rosenlinks.com/RTYCU/Ency

INDEX